Thank Our Lucky Stones

Mary Loretta McGillis

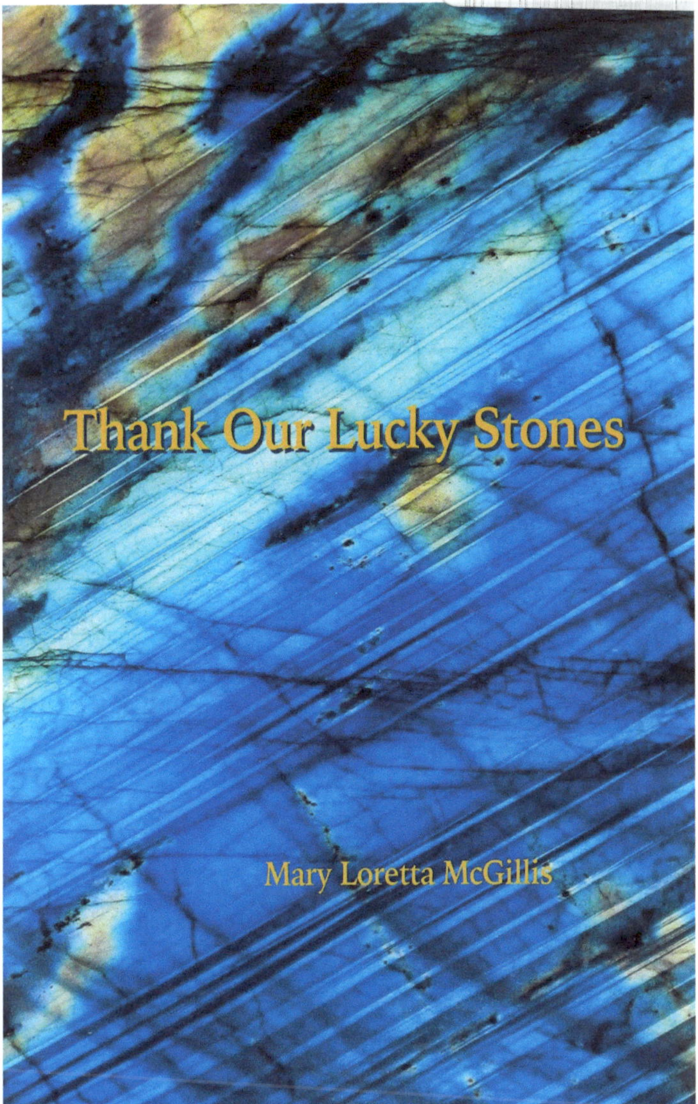

Find out how to discover your lucky *Soul Stone* in *Thank Our Lucky Stones!*

In this book, you will discover your Soul Stone and find your other 12 personal lucky stones for your pleasure or for your use as tools of empowerment.

The beliefs, wisdom, knowledge and customs regarding stones and stone lore prevalent in Celtic and other nations throughout ancient history and right up to these precious present times help us to choose stones that resonate with our soul. Stone legends have been left for us by our ancestors to help us on our journey here.

What are the legends? What are the properties of stones? Do stones really protect us, help us to heal and attract good fortune? You bet your lucky stone they do!

Thank Our Lucky Stones

Copyright © 2018 by Mary Loretta McGillis
Editing by Tara Molson

With written prior permission of the author, parts of the publication may be reproduced. All rights reserved in all media.

ISBN: 978-0-9939824-3-9 Published in Canada 2018

9th wave publishing

Table of Contents

What's Inside This Wee Book? 7

Chapter 1: Where to Begin? 8
How Do I Choose a Stone? 8
How Many Stones Do I Need? 9
Raw Stones 10
Caring for Your Lucky Stones 11
Charging Your Lucky Stones 13
Wearing Your Lucky Stones 14
Using Stones 15

Chapter 2: Astrology & Our Lucky Stones 16
What is a Birthstone of Month? 16
Pre-Gregorian Birthstones 17
Modern Birthstones 18
Ancient Birthstones 19
Ancient & Modern Birthstones 20
A Greek Legend 32
What Are Your Astrological Birthstones? 34
Linda Goodman & Star Sign Stones 36
Your Moon Sign and Your Rising Sign 37
Sun Sign Stones 38
The Day of the Week You Were Born 50
Seven Ruling Planets Chart 51
What Were the Stones of the Ancestors? 53

Chapter 3: Stone Legends 54
Monday's Child Rhyme 54
Thank you, Flora White 62
Lighted Stones 63
Left-handed or Right-handed Stones? 68
What is it about that Spiral? 69
Amulet versus Talisman 70
Stones of the Seas 71
Adder Stones 72

Jasper: Supreme Comforter..73
Legend of Labradorite 74
Home of the Northern Lights 75
Cairngorm ~ Smokey Quartz 76
Stone of Intuition: Fluorite 77
Nine of Diamonds..78
Stone of Peace: Diamond...79
Pictish Symbol Stones...80
A Few More Pictish Carvings, Just Because....................81
Four Jewels of the Tuatha Dé Danann 82
The Stone of Destiny in Ireland 84
The Stone of Destiny in Scotland...................................86
What is a Cairn?..87
The Standing Stones of Stenness...................................88
The Odin Stone 89
The Ring of Brodgar 90
Skara Brae...92
The Callanish Standing Stones 93
Giant's Causeway..94
Stone Carvings at Rosslyn Chapel 96
The Witch's Stone 98
World Heritage Sites 99
Newton and Colour and Notes....................................100
Do Colours Matter When Choosing a Stone?..............101
Frequency and Colour 102
Music and Sound and Stones in the Healing Arts..........103

Chapter 4: Stones for You.. 104
Helping Stones for Challenges.....................................104
A Selection of Stones to Begin....................................105
Challenges in Alphabetical Order................................122

Chapter 5: Your Soul Stone and Your Other Stones .. 128
List of My Personal Stones 129
Amergin and Brigit...130
A note from Mary McGillis...136
Need A Speaker? Conference Facilitator?...................137

In the 1970s, no one was talking much about heritage where I grew up in Peterborough, Ontario, Canada. We were creating a Heritage of Partying. That is another story. This story, the story of stones, is from the beginning of time and I wrote down these tales to remind me in later years and to inspire others to look to Our Lucky Stones for help.

There is no page on St. Hildegard of Bingen and her healing stones and sacred music in this book, but I mention her here to bring light to the fact that there is much to learn about stones and how they can help us all.

Please enjoy the book!

Love, peace, joy & happiness to you and yours,

Mary Loretta McGillis

P.S. There are four pages (PDFs) in this book that may be downloaded for free from celticconnection.ca by anyone, but it is only in reading the book that you will know all about discovering your soul stone and the other 12 stones that specifically will help you!

What's Inside This Wee Book?

Stone lore is celebrated in these pages. Discover the protective, healing and magical qualities of our lucky stones. Many early beliefs and customs prevalent among Celtic and other nations persist today. Here are some ideas to inspire and empower you!

Looking for love?

Looking for luck?

Looking for healing?

Looking for prosperity?

Looking for fertility?

Looking for weight loss?

Looking to buy a necklace, pendant or ring for the special person you love? Be sure to get the stone that matches their astrological sign or the month they were born or the day they were born … or even to help them with a challenge they may be experiencing!

Chapter 1: Where to Begin?

How Do I Choose a Stone?

If you see a stone and have to take it home with you, the beautiful Lakefield octogenarian and unique gemstone necklace maker June Helwig says, "You didn't choose the stone, it chose you."

raw rose quartz attracts pure love

Learn to feel the energy; there are several ways, so choose one or more of the following techniques to see which one resonates with you:

- Pass your hand over and feel the energy
- Put the stone in your left hand (receives) and feel the stone energetically
- Some people hear them (crystal hum)
- You may keep going back to one in your mind
- Choose the properties for which the stone is known

opal energizes

How Many Stones Do I Need?

There are many stones to choose, but only one you need ... by the end of this book, you will discover your Soul Stone!

1. Birthstone of month (ancient)
2. Birthstone of month (modern)
3. Birthstone of astrological sun sign
4. Birthstone of moon sign
5. Birthstone of rising sign
6. Stone for day of week
7. Stone of intuition
8. Stone of abundance
9. Stone of cleansing
10. Stone to overcome challenge
11. Stone of empowerment: decision stone
12. Stone of peace
13. Soul Stone

There is no precious gem that does not draw powers from the upper spheres.

Raw Stones

STONES IN A RAW STATE are not compromised; yet all stones (tumbled/cut) carry the essence of the original stone, no matter the size or whether tumbled or raw. When you do choose any stone, it's all about preference and experience and about considering the feelings you get when you first see or feel the stone.

spirit quartz

tourmaline

amethyst geode

Caring for Your Lucky Stones

There are countless ways to purify, bless, cleanse, so choose one or create one that resonates with you ~ simply your intention to cleanse will work. Cleansing techniques include using other stones, herbs, plants, trees, water, feathers, songs, ... any smoke, running water over the crystal with intention/prayer; asking angels/guides; sea salt and reiki, therapeutic touch, mind; sound, crystal bowls, drums, tuning fork, sunlight, moonlight & burying in the ground.

smoke to cleanse

Popular today: using an abalone shell or a cast iron vessel, burn sage or burn palo santo (holy wood from South America) and hold stones over top as the smoke drifts upward to purify the air and your crystals ...

In Ancient Greece, after fasting and silence, sulphur and minerals and such oils were used to cleanse and smudge special stones or objects. To North American natives, one of their four sacred plant medicines like sage, sweetgrass, and/or tobacco or cedar may be used. Or a Scottish lass may take a sprig of Juniper to burn and clear her home. An Irish colleen may sweep out any heated conversation with a broom and intent.

Many traditions around the world have similar ritual to clear negative energy, to cleanse or to bring vision. Smoke is known as a carrier of prayers or message to the Otherworld and smells may trigger visions.

 *abalone shell*

With your personal lucky stones, keep them all happy by storing or displaying them with a citrine stone. A citrine carries the essence of sunshine, known to cleanse all stones and to bring happiness. Another way to cleanse is to run water over them or to put your stones outside in the moonlight (some people do this every full moon for full power). Also, you may want to bury them in the ground for a regeneration with Mother Earth and/or intend for the stones and your space to be cleansed/purified/happy! Intention and expectation are huge, aren't they!

 *the happy stone: citrine*

Charging Your Lucky Stones

AFTER YOU CLEANSE THE STONE, you charge it!

Stones have consciousness; they are a part of Mother Earth. After you cleanse one, the stone will sleep and you awaken it by charging it; then program it!

Yes, talk to your stone. Charge it and program it at the same time! An example of what you may say, "I am charging you to send healing vibes all through this room." (And a "please" never hurts!)

Charge your stones to amplify any healing properties while thinking of them and intending that they will help you or someone else. For example, all quartz are known for their amplification properties; and while charging a clear quartz, you may put any intention into the stone: love and a peaceful feeling ~ then the stone will emanate these properties in a room.

Placing stones in sunlight or moonlight or running cool water over stones helps make them happy; read up on each one, though, because amethyst doesn't like the sunshine (she will fade)!

Wearing Your Lucky Stones

Adorn yourself with your stones!! Make your own luck!

Need Help Choosing Which Stone Is Right for Today?

Best Way to Wear Your Lucky Stone

Start wearing your birthstone and keep notes on how your life improves!

- *wear on your finger*
- *carry your lucky stones in a purse and connect by touching*
- *carry in pocket, bra, car or make a special place in your home to visit them*
- *wear as a pendant, necklace (talisman/amulet)*

Using Stones

GRIDS are a great way to charge stones. There is no wrong way to make a grid, but start with an intention: why you are making the grid ... to attract prosperity ... abundance ... to protect your home. Choose a pattern based on sacred geometry, or any pattern. These are great first steps; and when you make stone grids of different patterns with a variety of stones, the grids will help you with your intentions.

Once you have your space ready (table, floor, stones all about), place the central stone (remember quartz is the biggest amplifier on the planet) and follow your chosen pattern or intuition to place stones.

WHICH STONES ATTRACT MONEY? LOVE?

A GRATITUDE GRID!

GRATITUDE (KEY TO LIFE) HELPS your life in every way: when in a state of gratitude, you shift immediately to the power of pure love. Gratitude is a conduit to access the power inside you and your stone grid will help you focus and attract help.

'count your blessings and they will multiply'

Chapter 2: Astrology & Our Lucky Stones

What is a Birthstone of Month?

Different cultures have traditional stones associated with the birthstone of the month. Here are yours:

1. **Birthstone of Month (Ancient)**

2. **Birthstone of Month (Modern)**

Which stone is my stone?

Traditionally, birthstones are associated with every month. For example, the ancient birthstone for July is a moonstone while the birthstone on most modern charts feature the ruby for July.

Does this mean there are two possible birthstones of the month for everyone? Yes! You may choose the ancient birthstone for the month you were born or you may choose the modern birthstone of the month, or both!

If you wear your birthstone on jewelry or carry it with you, the wearing of it will bring you luck.

According to legend, birthstone healing powers are heightened during its assigned month.

 raw aquamarine

Pre-Gregorian Birthstones

Wearing the gemstone associated with your month of birth is a time old tradition that has been popular in many cultures since ancient times. The gems we now associate with *birthstones* are taken from the months of the Gregorian calendar year.

rose quartz   *snowflake obsidian*   *ruby*

These precious stones range from lovely red rubies and gorgeous green emeralds as seen in birthstone charts… but what of the stones of the Ancient Celts and the Ancestors of the Celts (or other indigenous tribes)? We know the Celts, and even the Picts, wore talismans and amulets and suspect that they had as much interest in stone lore as modern-day people.

picture jasper   *unakite*   *rutilated quartz*

Modern Birthstones

Modern Birthstones

January: garnet

February: amethyst

March: aquamarine

April: diamond

May: emerald

June: moonstone

July: ruby

August: peridot

September: sapphire

October: opal

November: citrine

December: turquoise

What is YOUR modern lucky stone?

free download of this page @celticconnection.ca

Ancient Birthstones

Ancient Birthstones

January: malachite

February: garnet

March: bloodstone

April: sapphire

May: red agate

June: pearl

July: moonstone

August: sardonyx

September: aquamarine

October: pink tourmaline

November: yellow topaz

December: blue topaz

What is YOUR ancient lucky stone?

free download of this page @celticconnection.ca

Ancient & Modern Birthstones

APRIL

April Ancient Lucky Stone: Sapphire

April Modern Lucky Stone: Diamond

MAY

May Ancient Lucky Stone: Red Agate

May Modern Lucky Stone: Emerald

JUNE

June Ancient Lucky Stone: Pearl

June Modern Lucky Stone: Moonstone

JULY

July Ancient Lucky Stone: Moonstone

July Modern Lucky Stone: Ruby

August

August Ancient Lucky Stone: Sardonyx

August Lucky Modern Stone: Peridot

September

September Ancient Lucky Stone: Aquamarine

September Modern Lucky Stone: Sapphire

OCTOBER

October Ancient Lucky Stone: Pink Tourmaline

October Modern Lucky Stone: Opal

NOVEMBER

November Ancient Lucky Stone: Topaz

November Modern Lucky Stone: Citrine

DECEMBER

December Ancient Lucky Stone: Blue Topaz

December Modern Lucky Stone: Turquoise

January

January Ancient Lucky Stone: Malachite

January Modern Lucky Stone: Garnet

FEBRUARY

February Ancient Lucky stone: Garnet

February Modern Lucky Stone: Amethyst

MARCH

March Ancient Lucky stone: Bloodstone

March Modern Lucky stone: Aquamarine

A Greek Legend

The gods decided that each sign of the zodiac needed a stone to build a strong connection with the people born under the sign. These stones would support the strengths of the zodiac signs by compensating for any weakness.

Astrological legends abound from all over our world

The conquest of Asia by Alexander the Great exposed the Greeks to the cultures and cosmological ideas of Syria, Babylon, Persia and central Asia. Western astrology came to Rome through the Greeks who identified Babylonian (Mesopotamian) origins: the Chaldeans and other cultures throughout the world study the cosmos: Sumerians, Babylonians, Armenians, Egyptians, Mayan, Hindu, Chinese, and there are many biblical references to the stars.

ASTRONOMY is the study of stars, planets, comets, and galaxies in our universe

whereas

ASTROLOGY is the study of the interpretation of these

IN WESTERN ASTROLOGY, and formerly astronomy, the zodiac is divided into twelve signs. Zodiac is a Greek word meaning 'circle of little animals', because of the many animals and mythological hybrids among the 12 signs of the zodiac corresponding to the constellations Aries, Taurus, Gemini, Cancer, Leo, Virgo, Libra, Scorpio, Sagittarius, Capricorn, Aquarius and Pisces.

can you find your zodiac animal, sign & constellation?

The special stones associated with constellations, stars and planets are your birthright, your lucky stones!

What Are Your Astrological Birthstones?

YOUR ASTROLOGICAL BIRTH CHART (natal chart) is a map of the position of the stars and planets when you were born. Some cultures look to your birth chart as a map of your life, because the interpretation of it holds the promise and potential of how you might live out your life.

As well as the ancient and modern birthstones of the month, you may also choose three additional stones associated with the day you were born: everyone has three 'signs' according to your birth (natal) chart: your three personal signs include your astrological birthstone SUN SIGN (virgo, leo, etc) and you also have a MOON SIGN and a RISING SIGN (ascending).

Sun Sign
aka primary sign, astrological or zodiac sign
defines your personality

'What sign are you?' Most of us know of our 'Sun' sign (which constellation the sun was in when you were born), because the twelve signs of the zodiac are well known dividers of the year.

From this section of the book, you have found your lucky stones for your Sun Sign.

SUN, MOON & RISING SIGNS define our
personality: they influence our individuality,
our patterns and behavior. 'Knowing thyself'
is the first step in understanding ourselves
and others and allows us to choose to change.
Think of little yellow sticky note papers pasted
all over you, defining you: 'procrastinator', 'lover'
'peaceful', 'successful', 'bitter', 'grieving'; and only
you can take off a sticky and replace it with a new
one!

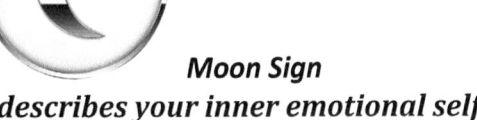

Moon Sign
describes your inner emotional self

Defines, describes, influences ... these words are chosen here for you to consider that your star chart is a map for you to interpret and any trait you find in words about your astrological sign are words you may choose to take on as your own, or not! Free will reigns on earth.

A^{SC} ***Rising Sign: The Ascendant***
influences your outer self/mask you show world

'The stars incline, they do not compel...we're moved like pawns on a chess board in the game of life... but by using free will ... anyone can change his character, control his environment and the attitudes of those close to them. When you become self-empowered, knowing about the map of your destiny, you become a mover and shaker in your life, not a pawn.' *Linda Goodman*

Linda Goodman & Star Sign Stones

Linda Goodman* had her own choices for stones & Star Signs:

Aries: Ruby

Taurus: Sapphire

Gemini: Aquamarine

Cancer: Moonstone & Pearls

Leo: Topaz

Virgo: Green or White Jade

Libra: Opal

Scorpio: Bloodstone

Sagittarius: Turquoise

Capricorn: Diamond & Onyx

Aquarius: Mixed Azurite & Malachite

Pisces: Emerald & Amethyst

*Linda Goodman ~ the first to write a bestseller book on astrology

Stonehenge, England

Your Moon Sign and Your Rising Sign

Have your natal chart drawn to find out your Moon Sign and your Rising Sign ... many sites online offer free birth charts or natal charts, even if you do not know your exact time of birth!

a natal chart, or birth chart, shows an exact moment in time

In the West, Moon signs and Rising signs are not as well known, simply because you must know the time and place of your birth to have your birth chart done. Your Moon sign, the position of the Moon in the sky at your time of birth, depends upon the time and place of your birth. A third sign is your Rising sign, or your Ascending sign ... what is coming over the horizon at the time of your birth. A Virgo may have Cancer as a Moon sign and Gemini ascending over the horizon as her Rising sign... and each of these signs/constellations have stone representations which you may use for your own personal stones!

Learning about astrology and what the map of your life looks like is an empowering endeavour.

Sun Sign Stones

Sun Sign Birthstones, according to astrology or the zodiac, are the stones associated with the planet ruling at the time of your birth (your sun sign).

If you wear your birthstone on jewelry or carry it with you, the wearing of it will bring you luck.

ARIES

THE RAM

MARCH 21 - APRIL 19
PLANET: MARS

PLANET STONE: RUBY

TAURUS
The Bull

April 20 - May 20
Planet: Venus

Planet Stone: Emerald

Gemini

The Twins

May 21 - June 20

Planet: Mercury

Planet Stone: Amethyst

Cancer

The Crab

June 21 – July 22

The Moon

Planet Stone: Pearl

LEO

THE LION

JULY 23 – AUGUST 22

THE SUN

PLANET STONE: RUBY

VIRGO

The Virgin

August 23 – September 22

Planet: Mercury

Planet Stone: Amethyst

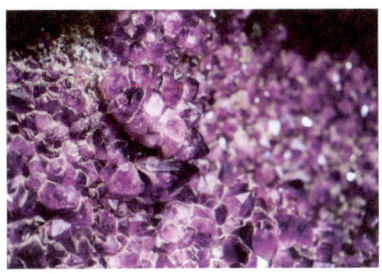

Libra

The scales

September 23 – October 22

Planet: Venus

Stone: Emerald

Scorpio

The Scorpion

October 23 - November 21

Planet: Mars

Stone: Ruby

Sagittarius

The Archer

November 22 – December 21

Planet: Jupiter

Planet Stone: Topaz

Capricorn
The Goat

December 22 - January 19

Planet: Saturn

Planet Stone: Turquoise

Aquarius

The Water bearer

January 20 – February 18

Planet: Uranus

Planet Stone: Diamond

Pisces

Two Fishes

February 19 – March 20

Planet: Jupiter

Stone: Yellow Topaz

The Day of the Week You Were Born

A special stone for your special day!

Zeller's Algorithm

Ever wonder what day you were born? Well, if you don't know, you can find out online. Zeller's Algorithm can be used to determine the day of the week for any date in the past, present or future, for any dates between 1582 and 4902.

Solar System

Seven Ruling Planets Chart

The day of the week you were born reveals more luck for you!

Ancient Babylonians created a seven day calendar wherein each day corresponded to one of the seven planets or celestial objects in the sky that could be seen with the naked eye.

With this chart, when you know which day you were born, you will discover the stone for your birth date, its trait, your planet or celestial object and the number associated with the planet! Remember to mark all your special, personal stones at the end of this book on your personal chart on page 129.

Day	Stone	Trait	Planet	#
Monday	Selenite	calms	Moon	2
Tuesday	Amethyst	heals	Mars	9
Wednesday	Emerald	loves	Mercury	5
Thursday	Sapphire	courage	Jupiter	3
Friday	Turquoise	lucky	Venus	6
Saturday	Onyx	protects	Saturn	8
Sunday	Ruby	empowers	Sun	1

Celtic Celebration Stones

Excavation finds in Europe dating over 10,000 years ago offer proof of the existence of a calendar system based on the phases of the moon and seasons: observing the solar solstices.

Each time of year features a stone with properties admired by the ancient Celts: look for the stone featured around the time of your birth or one that resonates with you.

Celts followed a solar year and a lunar month with the year divided into six months summer (light half) & six months winter (dark half).

What Were the Stones of the Ancestors?

The year began with winter on Samhain, (October 31/November 1), lasting until the end of April as the dark half of year, and the light half of year lasted from the 1st of May to the end of October.

Stones for each part of the year:

RED JASPER: New Year: Samhain: Yellow Topaz Beginning of Dark half of year, October 31st

GARNET: Winter Solstice (Yule): Garnet, around December 21st Shortest daylight of year, Garnet helps through long winter months of reflection

AMETHYST: Imbolc (February 1st) Feast of Goddess/St. Brigid; First day of Spring: Amethyst

TOPAZ: Spring Equinox (Ostara) First Day of Spring, around March 21st

SAPPHIRE: Beltaine (May 1st): beginning of light half of the year

PEARL: Summer Solstice (Litha): First Day of Summer, around June 21st

RUBY: Lammas (August 1): Ruby Beginning of the Harvest Time

SMOKEY QUARTZ: Autumn Equinox (Mabon): Smokey Quartz First Day of Autumn, around September 21st

Ancestral Stones at a Glance: Choose the stones that resonate with you that are featured near your birthdate:

Garnet	**Amethyst**	**Topaz**	**Sapphire**
Pearl	**Ruby**	**Smokey Quartz**	**Red Jasper**

Chapter 3: Stone Legends

Monday's Child Rhyme

THE OLD NURSERY RHYME about the days of the week is supposed to tell your character or future based on the day you were born is for fun, but the original has some bad days; time for a remake!

Monday's child is fair of face
Tuesday's child is full of grace
Wednesday's child is full of woe
Thursday's child has far to go
Friday's child is loving and giving
Saturday's child works hard for a living
But the child that's born on the Sabbath day
Is bonny, blithe and good and gay.

Originally based on ideas about the planets, consider the other traits of the planets not mentioned in the old days of the week rhyme and the fact that we all carry the love gene and unlimited potential.

Monday's child is lovely and calm
Tuesday's child is brave like no other
Wednesday's child is a charming talker
Thursday's child is lucky and wise
Friday's child laughs and loves
Saturday's child is full of joy
And Sunday's child is either …
      a wonderful Girl or a wonderful Boy!

Monday

IS ruled by the Moon and this means that a child born on a Monday will feel their emotions more than others. Strongly guided by their emotional center, even if they do not show that side so much, the sensitive Monday's child is kind.

Monday's child is the peacemaker of the days

Monday's lucky number: 2

OLD: MONDAY'S CHILD IS FAIR OF FACE.

NEW: MONDAY'S CHILD IS BEAUTIFUL.

TUESDAY is ruled by the planet

Mars (Martis in Latin). Mars is all about energy, so Tuesday's child is always on the go. *'Tuesday's child is full of grace: being in a state of grace allows for a direct conduit with God.'* How to maintain that grace you are born with? Gratitude! Born leaders and big dreamers.

Tuesday's child is braveheart of the days

Tuesday's lucky number: 9

OLD: TUESDAY'S CHILD IS FULL OF GRACE.

NEW: TUESDAY'S CHILD IS BEAUTIFUL.

WEDNESDAY is ruled

by planet Mercury. (Mercurri in Latin) Mercury is the thinking planet, promoting skills in communication. Communication is key!

Wednesday's child is the charming communicator of the days

Wednesday's lucky number: 5

OLD: WEDNESDAY'S CHILD KNOWS HOW TO SEW.

NEW: WEDNESDAY'S CHILD IS BEAUTIFUL.

THURSDAY is ruled by the planet Jupiter (in Latin, Jovis).

If you were born on a Thursday, consider yourself to be very lucky. Everyone would do well to find out where Jupiter is on their birth chart and use that power to harness their true karmic destiny. When Thursday's child follows their destiny, they are kind and generous, sharing their luck!

Thursday's child is seeker of truth of the days

Thursday's lucky number: 3

OLD: THURSDAY'S CHILD HAS FAR TO GO.

NEW: THURSDAY'S CHILD IS BEAUTIFUL.

FRIDAY is ruled by the planet Venus,

representing a goddess of love and beauty. (Veneris in Latin). People born on Fridays love everything to do with love and are full of love. Isn't love grand? If you have questions about love, look to see where Venus is on your birth chart!

Friday's child is love child of the days

Friday's lucky number: 6

OLD: FRIDAY'S CHILD IS LOVING AND GIVING.

NEW: FRIDAY'S CHILD IS BEAUTIFUL.

SATURDAY is ruled by the planet Saturn, the taskmaster of all of the planets. We all know Saturday is a great day for getting things done. Remember, though, after you get the jobs done, there is always time for fun! Driven and wise, know joy through experience.

Saturday's child is the joyful one of the days

Saturday's lucky number is the magical 8

OLD: SATURDAY'S CHILD WORKS HARD FOR A LIVING.

NEW: SATURDAY'S CHILD IS BEAUTIFUL.

SUNDAY is ruled by the sun.

The sun, even though is not an actual planet, it is the biggest light in the sky (one million Earths could fit inside the sun!) The sweetest people are born on Sunday ... they are wise and good and carry the joy and light of the sun wherever they roam. Creators of the days.

Sunday's is the amazingly creative child of the days

Sunday's lucky number: 1

OLD: BUT THE CHILD THAT'S BORN ON THE SABBATH DAY
   IS BONNY, BLITHE AND GOOD AND GAY.

NEW: SUNDAY'S CHILD IS BEAUTIFUL.

Thank you, Flora White

THE ART OF FLORA WHITE has
been a huge delight for over a hundred years! Thank you, Flora, for following your dreams and creating beauty while you were here ... here's wishing you good luck, and plenty of it, wherever you may be!

Lighted Stones

THERE ARE STONE LEGENDS IN EVERY CULTURE around the world and many of them are about stones that seem to have light in them. Some cultures have a name for the moving light inside stones: the spirits of the stone ...

LIGHT AT SUNSET

Carnelian: energizer

SUNSHINE

Citrine: happy

DAY LIGHT

Clear Quartz: healer

RAINBOW

Fluorite: intuition

Northern Lights

Labradorite: grounding

Fire

Sunstone: purifies

Moonbeam

Moonstone: balances

LIGHTNING

Opal: manifester

LIQUID LIGHT

***Selenite*:** calming

STARSHINE

***Star Sapphire*:** inspires courage

Left-handed or Right-handed Stones?

Two types of quartz crystals exist: left-handed and right-handed. In our world of duality, polarity, either left or right, clockwise or counter-clockwise, is apparent in stones, based on the directional growth of the stone.

Draw two spirals, one going to the left ... counterclockwise ... *unmaking or destruction* and the other going clockwise to the right, *making or creating* ~

AMMONITES, millions of years old and mainly found in the Rocky Mountains of Canada, are known as prosperity and/or protective stones; abundance all around. Spirals like the Fibonacci spiral are obvious in ammonites, yet found in all nature.

How powerful are you feeling today?

Pick out a stone to remind you of choice; a stone to remind that you hold the power of choice with every single decision you make every day.

The eastern yin yang symbol is found at the middle of the spirals at Newgrange and in the art of the Celtic weave. Are these messages from all of our ancestors and/or nature here to remind us to seek balance?

What is it about that Spiral?

... at Newgrange, Ireland

What do spirals have to do with stones? That same spiral is a part of every stone, a part of everything in nature.

WHEN YOU ARE SOUL SEARCHING and exploring your inner world, looking for who you are, you may end up seeing a hidden, monstrous part of you which lays dormant; instead of being scared by it, consider that dark as a strength inside that you didn't know you possessed, a tool to make you strong to defend yourself emotionally, physically, psychologically and spiritually. Think from a perspective that true power is choice, your strength will help you control and choose how and when you act or react.

Celtic weaves & symbols are found carved in stones and in art; they represent our interconnectedness to each other and to the planet.

Amulet versus Talisman

AN AMULET IS AN OBJECT with natural magical properties which people often use for protection and health. Amulets are reminders or tools to help us connect with our own energies: common amulets are stones, scarabs, shells, feathers and little figurines. In Ireland, flint arrowheads are preserved in museums and called 'elf-arrows'. Peasants would wear these flint arrowheads as amulets around their necks, to protect themselves from elf-shot.

Sharp shooter   *Amber Talismans*

Unlike a talisman, an amulet protects its owner. An amulet is meant to wear under clothes, away from stranger's sight.

... MAKE YOUR OWN LUCKY STONE/OBJECT

A TALISMAN IS an object, often a necklace or other jewelry, which must be charged with magical powers. You create it for a particular purpose by engraving an object and/or intending a reason for wearing it (may be for luck, for love, for health and/or for protection; or for any intention you desire.) Like Ted Andrews says in his great book *Animal Speak*: talismans have 'a suggestive effect on the mind.' (ie. They work!)

Stones of the Seas

Not all 'stones' are minerals, as there are many gem materials of organic origin, including pearls, amber and mother of pearl.

Abalone shells and pearls bring to mind the treasures discovered in the seas. These carry the essence of the waters. In a collection of stones, you may want to include abalone shells (for wearing or smudge pots); mother of pearl, freshwater pearls, pearls, mermaid's tears (sand washed glass) and ammonites (fossils), coral, larimar (the Atlantis stone), aquamarine, ocean jasper and, because of the connection between the moon and the sea, moonstone!

freshwater pearls

abalone shell

raw aquamarine

Adder Stones

Another sort of amulet is called Glein Naidr or the "adder stone". Some old Scots believed that the stone ensured good luck for the owner. In certain cases, the Highlander was known to travel long distances to seek holy water in which the Clach Bhuai was to be dipped.

The adder stones were known as magical gems or stones used by the druids, and which, when inspected by a chaste boy, would help him to see an apparition so as to foretell future events. (See Pennant's Tour in Scotland, 1769i, pp. 101, 102; 1774, third edition).

Stones formed naturally with a hole

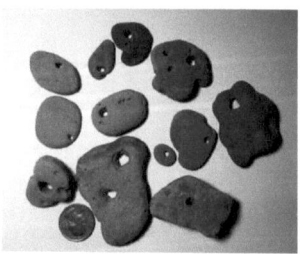

An adder stone, also known as hag-stone, witch-stone or serpents' egg, is a little stone usually found on a beach formed naturally with a hole running through it. These were thought to possess magical properties.

Jasper: Supreme Comforter

We all need a little tenderness, and what better than with a jasper stone? Everyone could use a Grandma Donnelly cup o' tea (not to mention her homemade buns!); but if she's not there at the moment, JASPER in the pocket helps! Just to give you an idea of the many kinds and colours of jasper:

Legend of Labradorite

Home of the Northern Lights: The Aurora Borealis: from Newfoundland & Labrador, Canada

Labradorite was named after the Canadian province of Newfoundland & Labrador since its discovery in the 17th century. Known as the home of the northern lights, there is an Inuit legend about the gemstone:

Once an Inuit warrior came upon a huge rock and saw that the northern lights were trapped inside. He broke open the stone and the northern lights escaped, yet some remained, and the stone became known as the beautiful labradorite.

Home of the Northern Lights

... speak to the lights ...

The Sami folk who follow the reindeer in the north, urge you to speak to the lights:

'Ask the lights to come and show themselves to you and offer a gift.'

The offer of exchange, a strong Celtic tradition, is respectful and acknowledges a relationship with the Otherworld.

Cairngorm ~ Smokey Quartz

The dark brown and black Smokey Quartz was called Morion and the yellow-brown to greyish brown stones were called Cairngorm after the Cairngorm Mountains where they were discovered in the Highlands of Scotland.

Known as powerful stones of grounding and protection, the Highlanders adorned themselves with Cairngorm brooches, kilt pins and stones on the handles of their weaponry, like the Scottish dagger sgian dubh, a "sock knife" which remains part of proper kilted apparel.

Smokey Quartz Crystal Point

Stone of Intuition: Fluorite

FLUORITE: Home of the rainbow; carries the essence of all healing stones. Intuition activator: reminds us of our magical world; reminds us to follow our heart & encourages positivity: helps you to balance life at one third work, rest & play!

Nine of Diamonds

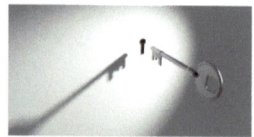 

THE NINE OF DIAMONDS is known as 'the curse of Scotland', because it was the playing card that Sir John Dalrymple wrote on to authorize the Glencoe Massacre on February 13, 1692, on the order of King William III. Thirty-eight men, women and children from Clan MacDonald of *Glencoe* were killed.

Glen Coe had been home to the MacDonalds since at least the early 14th century when they supported King Robert the Bruce. The chief of the MacDonalds of Glen Coe was Alasdair MacDonald, known as MacIain. He was a huge man with flowing white hair, beard and moustache. He was well respected by his own clan and feared by others - very much an old-school highland chief. Along with the chief, his wife was murdered that early morning; would King William III ever have imagined that a MacDonald ally would cut off the fingers of the clan chief's wife for her rings? Would King William ever have imagined that his God would condone this type of act after his 'Thou Shalt Not Kill' commandment? Sadly, similar atrocities continue around the world. How far we have strayed from our Garden of Eden. *If we do not remember our past ... or God?*

THE KEY TO POWER, true power, is when you conquer your emotions, when you choose to breathe before you act or re-act. Yay nine of diamonds and hurray to you for choosing an empowerment stone for peace. And hurray to you for knowing that, as an individual, you always have a choice. Are you going to add to the good of the world or the bad?

Stone of Peace: Diamond

LET'S BEGIN A HISTORY OF PEACE. *If we do not remember our past*, are we doomed to repeat it? All cycles in life repeat until we get the lesson. Let's say the Nine of Diamonds represents the **WORLD STONE**: the number **9** is all about completions and endings and **THE DIAMOND** (modern day) represents strength and love.

'diamonds are a girl's best friend' until she gets a Scottie dog

The Romans and Greeks believed that diamonds were the tears of the gods. Modern proof that diamonds make people happy: they bond relationships like marriage & speak love. The dark side of the mining of diamonds reminds us always of duality; let this stone represent a choice to remember the past and not repeat it.

THE PLAYING CARD WHICH once was used for a terrible purpose (ordering the massacre of a clan), can represent THE END of the terrible wars and atrocities that have taken place around the world for millennia. Yes, a card AND a stone for peace on earth.

It is our very personal choice to remember that this is our world and every single thing we do as an individual either adds to the good of the world or the bad. Choose a stone for your pocket to remember the lessons around the globe and then to ask for peace, feel peace, and be the peace you wish to see in the world.

Pictish Symbol Stones

Why did the Picts carve these symbols onto stones?

Is this a language?

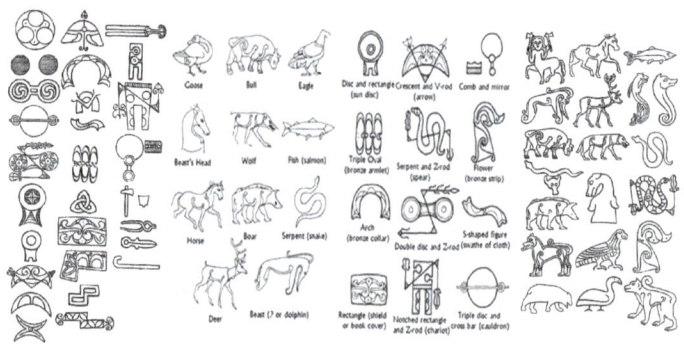

Did they all wear carved talismans or amulets?

A Few More Pictish Carvings, Just Because

the ferocity of the celtic wild boar

*the wisdom of salmon
a tuning fork & hieroglyph
of comb and mirror*

*pictish beast
(dragon) & hieroglyphs*

Four Jewels of the Tuatha Dé Danann

THE OLDEST DEITIES in Celtic mythology are the Mother of the Gods, the Goddess Danu, and the Dadga, the Good God of the *Tuatha Dé Dannan* (People of Danu).

In the legends, there are the tales of the gods arriving from the sky and of the treasures they brought with them... the stone of destiny is known as one of the four Jewels of the Tuatha Dé Danann. Brigid was the only goddess who came to Earth and the only one of the adventurers who returned to Heaven ...

The four jewels/treasures of the Tuatha Dé Danann:

The Dagda's Cauldron (the Good God, father of Brigid)
The Spear of Lugh
The Sword of Light of Nuada is known as
Claiomh Solais (pronounced Klee-uhv Sul-eesh)
And The Stone of Destiny aka **The** *Lia* **Fáil**

This book is dedicated to Brigit, who heard the Earth sing.

Heroes of the Dawn (1914)

Violet Russell & Elvery Beatrice

The Stone of Destiny in Ireland

Brigid says yes!

"We will take the four jewels: the sword of light, the cauldron of plenty, the spear of victory and the stone of destiny to build power, wisdom and beauty and lavish heartedness into the Earth."

Brigid took the **Stone of Destiny** in her hands and it shone like a white crystal and she laid the stone on the green grass where it sank into the Earth. A music played as it sank and suddenly all the hollows were filled with water, rivers and deep pools ... "It is the laughter of the Earth," said Ogma the Wise.

Ella Young, author of **Celtic Wonder-Tales, 1910**

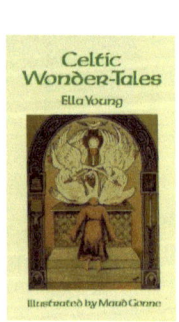 

The Stone of Destiny, Hill of Tara, Newgrange, Ireland

The Lia Fáil is the stone at the Inauguration Mound on the Hill of Tara in County Meath.

'From Failias was brought the Stone of Destiny, the Lia Fáil, which is at Tara, and would roar for the rightful King.'

The Yellow Book of Lecan, 1318: Vernam Hull, *The four jewels of the Tuatha Dé Danann.* vol 18, 73-89, Trinity College, Dublin.

The Hill of Tara, also known as The Hill of the King, or Teamhair na Ri in Irish, is located near the River Boyne near Navan in County Meath.

THE STONE OF DESTINY served as the coronation stone for hundreds of years for the High Kings of Ireland up until 500 AD. Legend tells that the stone would roar for the rightful King. It was from this stone that the *Tuatha Dé Danann* named Ireland 'Inis Fáil': Island of Destiny' in ancient times. 'Fianna Fáil' means 'soldiers of destiny.'

One of Ireland's most famous 'soldiers' was *Cú Chulainn* (pronounced Ke-Hullin). He appears in the mythologies of the Ulster Cycle as well as in Scottish and Manx folklore, and allegedly broke the stone with his sword when it did not speak for his buddy Lugaid. Maybe the stone did not like the circumstances of Lugaid's birth. Check out the old tales!

The Stone of Destiny in Scotland

The Scottish Crown Jewels & The Stone of Destiny

THE STONE OF SCONE, aka the Stone of Destiny is a powerful and ancient symbol of the Scottish monarchy, and has witnessed the coronation of its kings for hundreds of years. (These words courtesy of the official website of Edinburgh Castle).

In legends, the stone was used as a pillow by the Patriarch Jacob when he dreamed of Jacob's Ladder. Seen as a sacred religious object, it was believed to have been brought first to Ireland, then Scotland.

In 1296, Edward I of England took the stone from Scone and had it built into his own throne. Since then it has been used in the coronation ceremonies for the monarchs of England and then Great Britain.

On Christmas Day 1950, four Scottish students removed the stone from Westminster Abbey in London, England. Three months later, the stone turned up 500 miles away – at the front door of Arbroath Abbey.

In 1996, the stone was returned to Scotland and is now in the Crown Room at Edinburgh Castle with all the Honours of Scotland. The stone will only leave Scotland again when there is a coronation in Westminster Abbey.

What is a Cairn?

A CAIRN IS A human-made pile or stack of stones. There is a centuries old Scottish tradition of carrying a stone from the bottom of the valley and placing on top of an existing cairn, or adding a stone each time you visit a burial place.

The word CAIRN comes from the Scottish Gaelic word CÀRN (HEAP OF STONES). A cairn is said to have different purposes: to mark a grave, to mark a successful reaching of a summit, to mark a path or is known as a sea marker to help mariners.

THE CLAVA CAIRNS in the Highlands of Scotland are about 4,000-years-old and were built as a burial place along the east side of the River Nairn, close to Culloden Battlefield. The cemetery has remained a sacred place in the landscape for millennia.

The Standing Stones of Stenness

THE ORKNEY ISLANDS

The Standing Stones of Stenness stand around 19 feet tall, and are larger than the stones at the nearby Ring of Brodgar, about one mile northwest, all in northern Scotland.

Standing Stones of Stenness, Scotland

OTHER NEARBY MEGALITHS, which may have been part of the original complex, are the Watch Stone and the Barnhouse Stone.

The Watch Stone, with Ness of Brodgar in background

The Odin Stone

DESTROYED IN THE WINTER OF 1814, a holed monolith called the Odin Stone stood not far from the Standing Stones of Stenness in the far north end of Scotland. Another socket hole for a second megalith indicates that the Odin Stone was once one of a pair. Ancient lore of the Orcadian people share a tradition where young lovers would make an Odin Oath, an unbreakable oath when spoken at the Stone o' Odin.

An Orkney poem, *the Play o' da Lathie Odivere*, calls Odin "him dat hanged on da tree", referring to Norse mythology where the god Odin sacrifices himself on Ygdrassil, the world tree, and gains the knowledge of life, death and the rune stones.

GEORGE BERNARD SHAW: 'Better keep yourself clean and bright. You are the window through which you must see the world.'

The Ring of Brodgar

Canadian exchange student Tara Molson visits The Ring of Brodgar, a favourite of Dr. Patrick MacManaway.

DR. PATRICK MACMANAWAY, a practitioner of the healing arts, second-generation, training first with his parents at their Healing and Teaching Centre in Fife, Scotland, grew up as a neighbour and friend of the founders of Findhorn, Scotland. Patrick studied Medicine at Edinburgh University and then apprenticed in Western and Eastern approaches to landscape energy and traditional geomancy. He is a practitioner of earth acupuncture and geopathic stress remediation. Living half of each year in the United States and the other half in Scotland, he and Ivan McBeth co-founded Circles For Peace, a Vermont non-profit organization based on the philosophy that inner peace and inner strength can be restored by witnessing the rhythms and cycles of nature.

From the website of his friend and co-founder of Circles for Peace, Ivan McBeth (thank you, Fearne Lickfield):

'There are well over one thousand remains of stone circles still visible in Britain. They range from tiny ones a few yards in diameter, up to the Avebury megalithic complex that spans some eleven hundred feet. It is estimated that over 67 percent of these are true circles, 17 percent are flattened circles, and six percent are egg-shaped. There are a number of compound rings, of which the most advanced of all is at Avebury.

Avebury Megalithic Complex

THE ANCIENT STONE CIRCLE BUILDERS employed advanced geometry, had an intimate knowledge of astronomy, and were skilled as engineers. They could set out projects to an accuracy of one in a thousand (only an experienced surveyor with good equipment is likely to attain that accuracy, even today), and they could transport and erect blocks of stone weighing up to three hundred tons. They also knew of, and used the famous 3:4:5 right-angled triangle (also the 5:12:13, the 8:15:17, and the 12:35:37 right-angled triangles) in the setting out of ellipses, two thousand years before Pythagoras. Megalithic Man had an accurate solar calendar, and had set up a series of lunar observatories that could accurately observe the intricate 18.61 yearly cycle of the moon. He knew of the moon's "wobble" and could thereby predict eclipses, a massively complicated procedure even for modern man. He divided his year into sixteen parts, the cusps of which coincide with the Solstices, the Equinoxes, and the four fire festivals (Samhain, Imbolc, Bealtaine, and Lunasa) at the cross-quarters."

Skara Brae

IN THE WINTER OF 1850, a great storm blew the sand dunes and turf away and revealed the remains of a Stone Age village, Skara Brae. All of the buildings contained stone furniture and the village dates back over 5,000 years to what is known as the Neolithic period, when people first began to farm. The well-preserved ruins feature at least ten ancient dwellings with stone dressers, fish tanks and stone beds. About 400 metres away is Skaill House, built in 1620, long before the discovery of the village. Inside the house are the furniture and artifacts of generations of Skaill lairds, including a dinner service used by Captain James Cook on his final voyage.

The Callanish Standing Stones

The Callanish standing stones are on the Isle of Lewis, Scotland, and are a 5,000-year-old stone circle which appears on ancient Egyptian maps.

The Greek historian Diodorus Siculus was probably describing the ancient stone circle when he wrote:

'This island...is situated North and is inhabited by the Hyperboreans... And there is also on the island both a magnificent sacred precinct of Apollo and a notable temple which is adorned with many votive offerings and spherical in shape....

They say that the Moon, as viewed from this island, appears to be but a little distance from the Earth and to have upon it prominences like those of the Earth, which are visible to the eye. The account is also given that the God visits the island every nineteen years, the period in which the return of the stars to the same place in the heavens is accomplished.'

Giant's Causeway

Susanna Drury's View of Giant's Causeway: East Prospect, 1768

SCIENTISTS BELIEVE that the ancient formation of the Giant's Causeway, an area at the north-eastern tip of Northern Ireland where over 40,000 tightly placed basalt columns are packed together to look like an ancient manmade bridge, resulted from a volcanic eruption 60 million years ago.

Giant's Causeway

Finn McCool ~ Fionn Mac Cumhaill

THE LEGEND CLAIMS that Fionn mac Cumhail (Finn McCool the giant) built the Giant's causeway in order to walk over to Scotland to fight Benandonner, the Scottish giant. On the Scottish side of the causeway is the isle of Staffa, which has similar basalt formations at the site of Fingal's Cave. If you drew a line between the Giant's Causeway and Staffa, Iona sits on it and the mouth of Fingal's Cave looks towards Iona.

C. Cole, Engraved View of the Giant's Causeway, 1694.

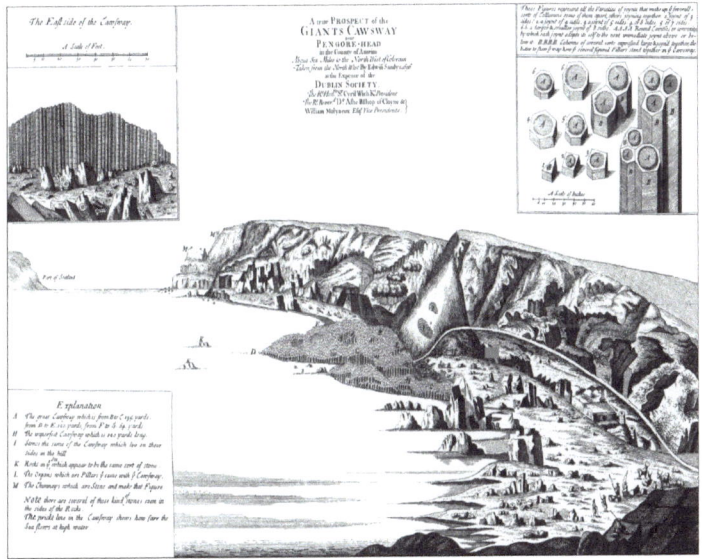

Stone Carvings at Rosslyn Chapel

STONE CARVINGS AT ROSSLYN Chapel, Scotland: The chapel is located in Roslin, seven miles South of Edinburgh, and was built by William Sinclair (or St. Clair) in 1446.

Rosslyn Chapel, Roslin, Scotland

There are elaborate stone carvings of angels, demons, roses, stars, elephants, pyramids, serpents and 110 carvings of the green man throughout the chapel.

The mystery of Rosslyn is why all of these seemingly pagan images appear in a place of Christian worship and why there has been a well-known connection of the small chapel to Freemasonry. Conspiracy theories abound about the Holy Grail, the Ark of the Covenant, the **Stone of Destiny** and secret chambers in the chapel.

The Apprentice Pillar at Rosslyn Chapel, Scotland

One ornate pillar, the 'Apprentice Pillar', was carved by a young apprentice to the master mason, who was overseas at the time of the carving. Upon his return, the master mason killed the apprentice in a fit of rage for having carved the stone.

The Apprentice Pillar features eight dragons at the base of the pillar, vine tendrils growing out of their mouths and up the pillar, representing the world tree.

The Latin inscription at the top of the pillar states:

"Wine is strong, a King is stronger, women are stronger still, but the Truth conquers all."

The Witch's Stone

THE WITCH'S STONE' AND PLAQUE: "Fear & fire: Janet Horne worked a lady's maid before she married, but by the year 1727 she was old and confused. Early that year, her neighbours reported that she was using witchcraft to turn her daughter into 'the devil's pony'. Janet and her daughter (whose hand was deformed) were imprisoned in Dornoch, where they were tried and found guilty of witchcraft. The daughter escaped before she could be punished, but her mother was sentenced to death. The next day, Janet Horne was stripped, rolled in tar and placed in a barrel. A grim procession carried her to this place, where she was burned alive. She was the last recorded person in Scotland to die in this terrible way."

The Janet Horne Sign at Dornoch, Scotland

Also on this plaque is a drawn picture of her at her trial with this quote: "I've tried to lead a good life, but my people are strangers to me now. My girl has a twisted hand and they whisper terrible things about us. Why do they hate us so?"

World Heritage Sites

Stonehenge, England

Sphinx, Egypt

Moai, Easter Island

A few of the many.

Newton and Colour and Notes

SIR ISAAC NEWTON AND COLOUR: In the 17th century, Sir Isaac Newton divided the spectrum into seven colours: **Red Orange Yellow Green Blue Indigo Violet**

Roy G. Biv: The rainbow colours are taught in schools with the acronym.

AND I SHALL SET THE RAINBOW IN THE SKY.
                                                                Genesis 9:13

Sir Isaac Newton chose the number seven for a mystical reason, not a scientific reason; based on an ancient Greek teaching that there was a connection between all colours, the musical notes, known objects in the universe and the chosen seven days of the week. Newton found colour is related to light is related to music: note the seven musical notes in a scale.

Do Re Mi Fa So La Ti

'If I have seen further than others, it is by standing on the shoulders of giants.'   Sir Isaac Newton

colour and light: colour has everything to do with light

Do Colours Matter When Choosing a Stone?

Red Orange Yellow Green Blue Indigo Violet

WHITE REPRESENTS ALL LIGHT whereas black represents the absence of light.

Both rainbow and chakra colours are of those same colours chosen by Isaac Newton to define the visible colours in the spectrum; they are ROY G. BIV.

Red Orange Yellow Green Blue Indigo & Violet, and they all vibrate at different frequencies, as do stones vibrate at different frequencies.

Frequency and Colour

ALL LIGHT TRAVELS at the same speed, but each colour has a different wavelength and each has a different frequency. The different wavelengths cause the colours of light to separate and become visible as they pass through a prism.

- shortest wavelength has the highest frequency
- longest wavelength has the lowest frequency red, orange and yellow are the warm colours
- green in the middle is the balancing colour
- blue, indigo and violet are the electric, cool colours

In keeping with the effects of light on the human body, red stimulates the immune system, yellow regulates digestion and green heals the lungs, heart and chest. Each color has its own frequency and has a healing effect on the organs that corresponds to different chakra colours.

tumbled stones to help you

Music and Sound and Stones in the Healing Arts

AS A YOUNG PERFORMING MUSICIAN, John Beaulieu noticed that some sounds and songs he played made people happy and some made them sad.

He went back to school and ended up writing *Music and Sound in the Healing Arts*. Since, he has gone on to teach about the use of tuning forks, stones and healing.

Find your personal stone, colour, frequency & note:

Stone	Colour	Frequency	Note
Jasper	Red	405-480 Thz	A
Carnelian	Orange	480-510 Thz	B
Citrine	Yellow	510-530 Thz	C
Emerald	Green	530-580 Thz	D
Turquoise	Blue	580-600 Thz	E
Sodalite	Blue	600-700 Thz	F
Amethyst	Violet	700-790 Thz	G

Chapter 4: Stones for You

Helping Stones for Challenges

DID OUR ANCESTORS and other tribes know that the rocks and herbs have properties to help us heal emotional, mental and physical issues? Would they advise us that some of the drugs we have been taking are only masking the problem and not helping us to get to the root of our ailments?

Crystals, gemstones, rocks ... these are powerful allies and are all non-invasive in our lives; here to stand beside us as a reminder of our connection to the planet, here offering help. Research and see if your ancestors knew about this kind of help that is there for us all!

As well as carrying a stone that will bring you good luck according to your birth chart and the day you were born, choose a stone to help with any challenge you are presently facing.

If you are looking to boost your energy, looking for luck, prosperity, contentment, pleasure... there is a stone for you! Some people carry in their pocket, put in their bra, wear on a necklace, bracelet or ring; you choose what makes you comfortable and have the benefits of your lucky stone with you all day, every day.

Stones, in the Highland traditions, are called Clach Bhuai or "The Powerful Stones" and were worn for protection and good fortune.

A Selection of Stones to Begin

assorted tumbled stones

In alphabetical order, the following list of stones, ones you already may know and love, are but a few of the beautiful stones you will discover on your own journey. There are many fascinating properties about thousands of stones in as many books ... enjoy!

ABALONE AND MOTHER OF PEARL

These two are interchangeable: abalone and mother of pearl are iridescent shells used for millennia for jewellery; and are both considered like the snail shell and also like the inner (nacre) coating of oysters and other mollusks.

Adder Stone

A stone with a natural hole in it (see Odin Stone, too); a lucky find on a beach, magical for you.

Agate

Agates are found in many colours (like jasper) and have similar grounding and stabilizing properties.

Amethyst

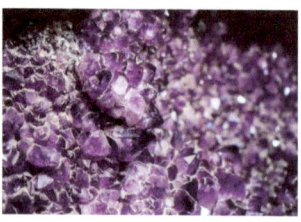

Great healing stone in general. Call any kind and any shade of amethyst into your addiction and see the violet flame transmuting the addiction to love.

Aquamarine

'Sea Water' is associated with the seas and mermaids; calming and protects on ocean voyages, cruises. A go with the flow stone, calms you on your journey to enlightenment.

Bloodstone

The Stone of Christ ~ the ancients said the wearer will be fortunate & rich ... aka the Warrior Stone as it helps with bleeding/blood.

Blue Lace Agate

A stone for speakers; inspires truth talking and peace.

Carnelian

Like citrine, carnelian carries properties to clear other stones; a great healing stone ... energizing! helps anything to do with the blood (pregnancy, digestion, heart)

Celestite

Heavenly and uplifting; brings clarity and calmness.

Chrysocolla

Cleopatra's wise stone helps you realize your dreams; soothes anger and transmutes to love.

Citrine

The abundance stone: cleanses all stones instantly, home of sunshine ... harnesses the power of the sun: the happy stone; stone of prosperity AKA the merchant's stone.

Coral

All colours of coral promote peaceful healing and also worn for protection.

Emerald

The love stone: promotes fertility and patience and is a protective stone. A stone of balance.

Fluorite

Home of the rainbow; fluorite carries the essence of all healing stones. Intuition activator: reminds us of our magical world; reminds us to follow our heart & encourages positivity: helps you to balance life at one third work, rest & play!

Fuchsite

Pronounced like book, fook-site, helps overcome past or any victim mode (blah-me/blame mode) to encourage accepting that you are responsible for fixing your life and confronting and overcome your negative habits. Create new positive habits. A lot of other stones will help with this as well; ask yourself which stones will encourage you to be responsible for creating a beautiful life for yourself; they help us to know we are creating our lives with every choice.

Garnet

Like St. Jude, garnet helps with hopeless causes and inspires faithfulness and loyalty: garnets are known as great heart stones and protect against depression. This is known to be the stone of love and health.

Gratitude Stone (the key to life): Choose a stone, any stone, to help you focus on being grateful.

Hematite

Grounds you, slows you to just be for a bit (great for a break from the do, do, do).

Jade

Jade is for good luck, prosperity and abundance. Also inspires peace and wisdom.

Jasper

Comforts & nurtures: helps overcome stress; helps to achieve harmony & balance in life, comes in many colours, types.

Labradorite

Named for the east coast of Canada, labradorite will protect and ground.

Lapis Lazuli

Enlightens and helps you to follow your true destiny; a wisdom stone.

Larimar

Found only in the Dominican Republic, thought to be the stone visionary Edgar Cayce predicted would be found where parts of Atlantis would resurface. 'The Atlantis Stone' promotes peace.

Malachite

Malachite helps pain, and the properties are known to reduce inflammation, the root of all disease.

Mookaite

Inspires passion and adventure; so when you feel like a quest (inner/outer), wear this stone!

Moonstone

Connecting the moon and the water, moonstone balances emotions, helps with clarity and is calming. A woman's stone, moonstone connects you to your divine feminine power and inner Goddess. Wearing a moonstone is like putting on your Goddess cloak. If you give your lover a moonstone on a full moon, the stone blesses your relationship.

Ocean jasper

A nurturing stone, it helps to wash away unwanted, negative feelings and increase positive thoughts. Carries the cleansing essence of the ocean.

Onyx

Both a protector and releaser: black onyx gives you confidence to let go of negative thoughts and to trust.

OPAL

Helps with manifestation of your thoughts: consider what you are wishing for when wearing an opal!

PERIDOT

A powerful stone of manifestation, also helps with clarity and focus. A stone of forgiveness.

Pyrite

Also known as fool's gold, pyrite will attract good fortune and protects.

Quartz

The master healing stone with so many uses: restores energy and harmony in the body.

Rhodochrosite

Empowers you by inspiring feelings of self-worth. A love thyself kind of feeling stone.

Rhodonite

Calms you and inspires you to connect with others.

Rose Quartz

Rose Quartz helps those grieving; a soothing stone. Attracts pure love and helps heal relationships.

Ruby

Wearing a ruby will help to bring the light into dark places; it promotes kindness and energy. The ruby also harnesses the power of the sun for love, passion and victory.

Rutilated Quartz

Protects from the electromagnetic smog emanating from computers and cell phones. Has properties that are similar to the stone shungite.

Sapphire

When exposed to the morning sun, sapphire brings prosperity. Known as the beloved stone of Saturn, legend says Saturn was the first planet to appear, bringing light out of the darkness. Brings courage.

Sea Glass (Mermaid's Tears)

Carries the essence of the seas ... glass ground down by sand and time.

Shungite

Detox your body, mind ... EMF protection here and purifier of water, too!

Smokey Quartz

The Protector: draws light into you to protect you; anchors and grounds you to the earth and helps grief.

Sodalite

The Stone of Truth, Artists and Musicians; grounding and inspires creativity.

Spirit Quartz

This amethyst grows in clusters and is healing; stops nightmares and bedwetting.

Tiger's Eye

Inspires courage and grounds you to your power.

Topaz

The topaz is said to bring joy and good luck to the wearer. Also symbolizes love, keeps your lover safe and encourages fidelity.

Tourmaline

Absorbs negative energy, protects your energetic field and is a powerful grounding stone.

Turquoise

Wearing this stone can help you give flight to your dreams: a good luck stone & protects. Boosts your ambition in a good way. Fortune follows the wearer of this good luck stone.

Challenges in Alphabetical Order

As well as carrying a stone that will bring you luck according to your birth chart and the day you were born, choose a stone to help with any challenge you are presently facing.

Looking for more energy, looking for luck, prosperity, good health, love, peace, joy, grounding, contentment, pleasure ... there is a stone for you!

Some people carry their lucky stone in their pocket, put in their bra, wear on a necklace, bracelet or ring; you choose what makes you comfortable and have the benefits of your lucky stone with you all day, every day.

AMPLIFIER/MASTER HEALER: clear quartz

ANXIETY: jasper, bloodstone, carnelian, citrine

ALIGNMENT: kyanite, tourmaline

ALZHEIMERS: rose quartz, carnelian, malachite

ARTHRITIS: labradorite, amethyst, malachite

ASTRAL TRAVEL: rutilated quartz, phantom quartz

BALANCE: kyanite, moonstone, clear quartz

ANGER: chrysocolla, jasper, amethyst

BLEEDING: bloodstone is also known as the warrior stone or Stone of Christ

BLOOD: carnelian, bloodstone, malachite

BONES: fluorite, malachite, rhodonite

CALMING: jasper, coral, celestite, amethyst

CANCER: rose quartz, any quartz, malachite

CHANGES: jasper, labradorite, clear quartz

CHILDBIRTH: carnelian, jasper, eagle stone (aetites), moonstone, spirit quartz, clear quartz

CHILDREN: crysocolla, carnelian

CLARITY: amber, selenite, celestite

CLEANSER: selenite, citrine, carnelian

COMFORTING; jasper, onyx, amethyst

COMMUNICATION: sodalite, clear quartz

CONFIDENCE: opal, jasper

COURAGE: tiger's eye, bloodstone, topaz, rose quartz

CREATIVITY: sodalite

DEPRESSION: selenite, quartz (rutilated, smokey, any quartz), jasper, carnelian, amethyst, fluorite

DEMENTIA: rose quartz, clear quartz, malachite

EMF BARRIER: Electromagnetic Field (produced by electrically charged objects like power lines, cell phones, computers, etc) which may adversely affect health ... these stones act as barrier/protection: rutilated quartz, shungite

ENERGY: carnelian, garnet, citrine

FEAR: jasper, charoite

FERTILITY: moonstone, spirit quartz

FORGIVENESS: selenite, rose quartz

FORTUNE & RICHES: bloodstone, citrine, jade

GRIEVING: selenite, rose quartz, smokey quartz

GROUNDING: labradorite, onyx, obsidian, sodalite

HEALING: amethyst heals addictions and transmutes negativity to love; rhodonite heals past traumas and moonstone calms emotions, leading to deep healing; fluorite carries the essence of all healing stones; and rose quartz attracts pure love to help with many issues including problems associated with breathing, heart, dementia, alzheimers, parkinsons; fuchsite 'the healer's stone'

HEART: carnelian, rose quartz, rhodochrosite

INFLAMMATION: malachite: malachite helps with inflammation, the root of all disease

INTUITION: fluorite, citrine, amethyst, rutilated/any quartz

JOY: citrine, turquoise

LACTATION: jasper, carnelian

LOVE: diamond, rose quartz, moonstone

LOVERS: moonstone calms emotions for deep healing

LUCK: jade, turquoise

MANIFESTATION: chrysocolla, clear quartz

MEDITATION: obsidian, moonstone, larimar, quartz

MUSICIANS: sodalite inspires creativity

NEGATIVITY: amethyst, violet flame transmutes to love

NIGHTMARES: spirit quartz, rose quartz

NURTURING: jasper, moonstone

OPTIMISM: pearl, citrine

PARKINSONS: quartz, amethyst, malachite, carnelian

PASSION: ruby, moonstone

PATIENCE: emerald, clear quartz

PEACE: selenite, jasper, larimar, jade, aquamarine, angelite

POSITIVENESS: amethyst, rose quartz, quartz

INNER TRAVEL: phantom quartz, rose quartz

PREGNANCY: moonstone, carnelian, jasper, quartz

PROSPERITY: citrine, jade, turquoise

PROTECTION: onyx, obsidian, labradorite, smokey quartz, bloodstone, tourmaline

RELATIONSHIPS: rhodochrosite, rose quartz

RESPONSIBILITY: fuchsite

REVITALIZING: carnelian, garnet, citrine

ROMANCE: sapphire, moonstone

SEASICKNESS: aquamarine

SECURITY: onyx, obsidian, tourmaline

SEXUAL ABUSE: sodalite, moonstone, chrysocolla, rose quartz, rhodochrosite

SEXUAL PROWESS: carnelian, ruby, moonstone

STRENGTH: garnet, tiger's eye

STRESS: any agate, amethyst, coral, quartz, jasper, celestite

SUCCESS: peridot, citrine

THROAT: any opal, turquoise, chrysocolla, malachite, blue lace agate

TRANSITIONS: jasper, labradorite, clear quartz

TRAUMA; obsidian, chrysocolla, rose quartz, clear quartz

TRUTH; blue lace agate, clear quartz

WEIGHT LOSS: malachite, fluorite, carnelian, quartz

WISDOM: jade, lapis lazuli, clear quartz

Which will you choose from your personal stones for today?

Chapter 5: Your Soul Stone and Your Other Stones

How to Discover Your Soul Stone

Step One
Your eyes are the windows to your soul.
Simply look in the mirror and you will see the colour of your soul shining through the windows of your eyes. Choose any stone representing that colour.

Now that you have an idea of which stone matches your eyes or resonates with you when thinking of the colour of your eyes and the colour of a stone, there is a second step to discover your Soul Stone.

Step two
What note are you here to sing? Open your mouth and sing 'ah' : your voice will drop into natural tone, your tone, which correlates to a colour for you to consider another stone.

If your eye colour matches your tone colour, you will find a Soul Stone of that colour that will resonate with you. In the case of two colours, listen to your heart and soul and a stone will choose you!

Everyone needs their Soul Stone...there is a lucky stone for everyone!

free download of this page @celticconnection.ca

List of My Personal Stones

List of My Favourite Personal Stones

1. Lucky Ancient Birthstone of Month: _____
2. Lucky Modern Birthstone of Month: _____
3. Sun Sign Birthstone: _____
4. Moon Sign Stone: _____
5. Rising Sign Stone: _____
6. Day of the Week Stone: _____
7. Stone of Intuition: _____
8. Stone of Abundance: _____
9. Stone of Cleansing: _____
10. Stone to Overcome Challenge: _____
11. Stone of Empowerment: _____
12. Stone of Peace: _____
13. Soul Stone: _____

free download of this page @celticconnection.ca

Amergin and Brigit

Amergin was the first Milesian to step foot on Ireland, and his famous 'Song of Amergin' was spake:

Amergin, Bard of the Milesians, lays claim to the Land of Ireland with the 'Song of Amergin':

I am a stag: of seven tines,
I am a flood: across a plain,
I am a wind: on a deep lake,
I am a tear: the Sun lets fall,
I am a hawk: above the cliff,
I am a thorn: beneath the nail,
I am a wonder: among flowers,
I am a wizard: who but I
Sets the cool head aflame with smoke?
I am a spear: that roars for blood,
I am a salmon: in a pool,
I am a lure: from paradise,
I am a hill: where poets walk,
I am a boar: ruthless and red,
I am a breaker: threatening doom,
I am a tide: that drags to death,
I am an infant: who but I
Peeps from the unhewn dolmen, arch?
I am the womb: of every holt,
I am the blaze: on every hill,
I am the queen: of every hive,
I am the shield: for every head,
I am the tomb: of every hope.

Song of Amergin translated by Robert Graves, from *The White Goddess *There are many beautiful versions of this translation.*

Here is an excerpt from Ella Young's *Celtic Wonder Tales* about the Milesians:

It was Brigit that was there to meet Amergin when he first arrived. The Tuatha De Danaan challenged him to take the Isle of Destiny from them:

Ogma, Nuada, and the Dagda, came to try them. "What people are you?" asked Nuada, "and from what country have you come?"

"We are the sons of Milesius," they answered; "he himself is the son of a god–even of Beltu, the Haughty Father. We are come from Moy More, the Great Plain that is beyond the horizon of the world."

"How got you knowledge of Ireland?" asked Ogma.

"O Champion," answered Amergin, "from the centre of the Great Plain there rises a *tower of crystal*. Its top pierces the heavens, and from the ramparts of it the wisest one among us got sight of this land. When he saw it his heart was filled with longing, and when he told us of it our hearts too were filled with longing. Therefore, we set out to seek that land, and behold we have come to it. We have come to Inisfail, the Island of Destiny."

"And ye have come to it," said the Dagda, "like thieves in the night; without proclamation; without weapon-challenge. Ye have lighted a fire here, as if this were a no-man's land. Judge ye if this be hero conduct."

"Your words have the bitterness of truth in them," said

Amergin. "Say now what you would have us do."

"You are a druid and a leader among your people," said Nuada. "Give judgment, therefore, between yourselves and us."

"I will give judgment," said Amergin "I judge it right that we should return to our ships and go out the distance of nine waves from the land. Use all your power against us, and we will use all our power against you. We will take the Island of Destiny by the strength of our hands, or die fighting for it!"

"It is a good judgment," said Ogma, "Get back to your ships! We will gather our battle-chiefs for the fight."

Ogma, Nuada, and the Dagda, went away then from the Milesians. The Milesians began to put out the fire they had kindled, and as they were quenching the embers, Brigit threw her mantle of power about her and came to the Milesians in her own shape. When Amergin saw her he knew that she was the Mighty Mother, and he cried out: "O Ashless Flame, put a blessing on us now, that our luck may not be extinguished with these embers."

"O Druid," said Brigit, "if you had wisdom you would know that before the First Fire is extinguished the name-blessing should be pronounced over it."

"O Mother of All Wisdom, I know it, but the name-blessing is gone from me. I met three queens as I came hither, and each one asked the name-gift of me. They were queens discrowned: I could not put refusal on them."

Brigit began to laugh then, and she cried: "O Amergin, you are not counted a fool, yet it seems to me that if you had much wit you would know the eyes of Brigit under any cloak in the world. It was I, myself, who asked the name-gift from you three times, and got it Do not ask a fourth blessing from me now, for I have blessed you three times already."

She stooped and lifted a half-quenched ember from the fire. She blew on it till it became a golden flame–till it became a star. She tossed it from one hand to the other as a child tosses a ball. She went away laughing.

The Milesians went back to their ships. They put the distance of nine waves between themselves and the land. The Tuatha De Danaan loosed the Fomor on them, and a mighty tempest broke about their ships. Great waves leaped over them and huge abysses of water engulfed them. The utmost power of the Milesians could not bring the ships a hair's breadth nearer to the shore. A terrible wind beat on them. Ireland disappeared. Then Amergin cried out:

"O Land, that has drawn us hither, help us! Show us the noble fellowship of thy trees: we will be comrades to them. Show us the shining companies of thy rivers: we will put a blessing on every fish that swims in them. Show us thy hero-hearted mountains: we will light fires of rejoicing for them. O Land, help us! help us! help us!"

Ireland heard him, and sent help. The darkness cleared away and the wind was stilled.

Then Amergin said:

"O Sea, help us! O mighty fruitful Sea! I call on every wave that ever touched the land. O Sea, help us!"

The sea heard him, and the three waves that go round Ireland–the wave of Thoth, the wave of Rury and the long slow white foaming wave of Cleena. The three waves came and lifted the ships to the shore. The Milesians landed.

The Tuatha De Danaan came down to make trial of their battlestrength. Hard was the contest between them. The Milesians held their own against the gods. When they saw that the Milesians could hold their own, the *Tuatha De Danaan* drew themselves out of the fight. They laughed and cried to the Milesians:

"Good heroes are ye, and worthy to win the earth: we put our blessing on you."

Nuada shook the bell-branch, and the glory that the *Tuatha De Danann* had in Tir-na-Moe before they ever set themselves to the shaping of the earth–that glory– came back to them. They had such splendour that the Milesians veiled their eyes before them.

"Do not veil your eyes!" said Nuada, "we will draw the Cloak of invisibility, the Faed Feea, about us. We give you Ireland: but, since our hands have fashioned it, we will not utterly leave the country. We will be in the white mist that clings to the mountains; we will be the quiet that broods on the lakes; we will be the joy-shout of the rivers; we will be the secret wisdom of the woods. Long after your descendants have forgotten us, they will hear our music on sunny raths and see our great white horses lift their heads from the mountaintarns and shake the night-dew from their crested manes: in the end, they will know that all the beauty in the world comes back to us, and their battles are only echoes of ours. Lift up your faces, Children of Milesius, Children of Beltu the Haughty Father, and greet the land that belongs to you!"

The Milesians lifted up their heads. No glory blinded them, for the *Tuatha De Danaan* had drawn the *Faed Feea* about themselves. They saw the sunlight on the grass like emerald fire; they saw the blueness of the sky and the solemn darkness of the pine trees; they heard the myriad sound of shaken branches and running water, and behind it echoed the laughter of Brigit.

Heroes of the Dawn (1914) Violet Russell & Elvery Beatrice

A note from Mary McGillis

Thank you for reading *Thank Our Lucky Stones*. If you enjoyed it, please take a moment to leave a review at your favourite online retailer anywhere, like Amazon USA, Amazon.ca or Amazon UK.

I would love to hear your stone stories (or any story you wish to share ... I love folklore)! At my website, you can contact me, sign up for my newsletter/blog to be notified of new releases, read my blog (please share!) and find me on social networking. THANK YOU for helping me to live my dream! Long may you run!

*NEW in 2018 ... her book *Thank Our Lucky Stones*

'An excellent new/old way to look at stones; and it is a visually stunning, informative and practical book for all stone aficionados ... LOVE the legends! I want more!'

Contact Info:

Facebook: CelticConnectionCanada

Twitter and Instagram: Celtic_Canada

Email: mary@celticconnection.ca

Celtic Connection, 25 Queen St, Box 69, Lakefield, ON K0L2H0

Websites:

marymcgillis.ca   **celticconnection.ca**

Need A Speaker? Conference Facilitator?

Mary McGillis lives in Peterborough, gateway to the Kawartha Lakes near Toronto, and has inspired the area with her Celtic Connection boutique, an urban Fairy and Dragon Trail and The Fairy and Dragon Festival. Has passport, will travel!

She writes about all things Celtic and other passions on her blog and in her books. For more about Mary McGillis and her Little People associations, email her at **mary@celticconnection.ca**. marymcgillis.ca ~ celticconnection.ca

www.ingramcontent.com/pod-product-compliance
Lightning Source LLC
Chambersburg PA
CBHW042335150426
43195CB00001B/2